<u>WHY</u> Are You <u>SO</u> Quiet?

The Year I Learned To Speak: Spoken Word 2025

WHY Are You SO Quiet?

The Year I Learned To Speak: Spoken Word 2025

Tristan Elliott

ISBN: 978-1-945489-21-1 (paperback)

Alight Press LLC
Eugene, OR 97405
www.alightpress.com
Printed in the United States of America

Table of Contents

Acknowledgements

My parents, Nancy and Scott Elliott, for their unconditional love and support.

Phosphor Emery Alethes for friendship, writing support, and guiding me to Wordcrafters.

Wordcrafters for giving me a writing home & making me feel valued as a person & as a writer.

My "writing parents"—Jorah LaFleur and Jeaux Bartlett—for seeing me and loving me in a way that made it safe to start to put down roots and emerge, answering my many questions and taking my anxiety texts and phone calls. Jorah for mentoring me through the art of spoken word and performance, and calling me a poet, so I had no choice but to be one. Jeaux, for providing me with a supply of hugs, gold stars, and encouragement that keep me writing, and for helping me with all the steps of publishing this book.

The hosts and poets at The Hybrid, Art City Open Mic, Eugene Poetry Club, and Eugene Poetry Seasons, for creating such inspirational spaces and always making me feel valued and welcomed.

Introduction

For my entire life, I have been shamed for being too quiet and not speaking enough. It is quite common for people that I don't know to make fun of or point out how quiet I am. Any time I go to a new group I dread the moment that I know is coming; when somebody will inevitably ask me—why are you so quiet? As if I owe them an explanation of my existence.

Ironically, people shaming me for being quiet led me to discover the art of spoken word poetry. I wrote my first spoken word piece, "<u>WHY</u> Are You <u>SO</u> Quiet," out of frustration for the way the world responds to me, without even really knowing what spoken word was, or that that's what I was creating. I just knew that what I had to say was bigger than the words on the page and that it wanted to be spoken.

Shaking in fear, I shared it at an open mic for the first time in March of 2025. I was very surprised when I was told that spoken word was for me and that performing it was a thing that I could do.

It has turned out to be not only a thing that I can do, but something that I am compelled to do and that the universe will make sure that I do, whether I like it or not.

Between that first open mic and the end of 2025, I spoke at almost forty events. I love that it gives me a creative outlet that facilitates connection with the audience. And best of all, nobody who has heard me do a spoken word piece ever tells me I am quiet!

I originally created most of my pieces in my head and scribbled down notes for myself to perform memorized, without ever intending to turn them into completed written poems. But, because people frequently ask me for written copies, I decided to publish a book of them for my one-year anniversary of stepping into the spoken word world.

Here are twelve of the many pieces that I wrote and performed over the year. They are all intended to be spoken, the stage adding depth that cannot be portrayed on the page.

<u>WHY</u> Are You <u>SO</u> Quiet?

(January)

on my way to Sunday service
minding my own business
somebody stopped me

why are you so quiet?
always lurking around here
ugh
they said

I knew before they spoke
by the way they looked at me
what they were going to say
because it's the same thing
people always say to me

Why are you so quiet?

and not in a
are you okay
kind of way

or an
I'd like to get to know you better
kind of way

but in a
what is wrong with you
kind of way

demanding an explanation
that will drain my resources
already depleted
from living in a world
that is not made for me
and does not want me

and before you argue with me
about that
let me tell you
the things that people say to me

I would rather die than be like you
if I were as quiet as you, I would kill myself
you should just kill yourself
weirdo
freak

monstrosity
how do you stand to be yourself?
God made a mistake in creating you
you can not be the way that you are

but that is the way that I am

the way I was made
and I must constantly justify my existence
defend my right to be
to breathe
to take up space
to move through spaces

the same spaces that fly rainbow flags
and hang black lives matter banners
touting inclusivity
but still questioning and shaming
those that can not adhere
to the known as neurotypical
but I say neurodominant
ways of being
including the so called
"normal" amount of speaking

because words
have become a required currency
in the false prosperity
that is actually extractive productivity
under white supremacist hetero patriarchal
capitalist hierarchy

I must fill the space
so you don't have to _feel_ the space
because what would happen
if you had space to feel?

feeling leads to questioning
your own discomfort
your own privilege
your own oppression

perhaps what would it take
to dismantle the system
that holds us all captive
that manufactures gucci purses
alongside genocides

the system can not allow that to happen

it must keep us all busy & chattering
to uphold it

so it can continue to pit us against each other
othering one another
because in order for it to maintain
some people
must always remain oppressed

so clearly
the most pressing issue of the times
while the earth is literally dying
is to ask me
why are you so quiet?

if I do try to explain
I'm dismissed anyway

too sensitive
attention seeking
drama queen
invalid way of being

I know how to perform
wear a mask

say this scripted poem
smile & nod
wait to cry until I get home

but do you know
that none of us are free
until we are all free

nobody is free until we are all free

and we are not yet free

in progressive spaces
it is no longer acceptable to say

why can't you walk?
why are you so fat?
why are you so queer?

if anyone dared to speak like that
someone
if not the entire room
would rise up & intervene
advocating on their behalf
that we welcome all people

and they do not have to explain
their existence
but

why are you so quiet?

only makes all eyes turn to me
turn on me
as if to say
yes, why are you so quiet?
I have been wondering the same

and the room closes in
frozen in place
icicles searing my throat
ensnaring my breath
encapsulating my voice
and nobody speaks for me

and then you wonder
why am I so quiet?

but the real question is
why are YOU so uncomfortable
with silence?

What God Can I Have?

(February)

when I was a kid
I had no God

not even something to question

no one I knew had one
so I just kept everything inside
until one day I exploded
screaming
WHAT GOD CAN I HAVE?
and how do you find one?

Is God a sunrise?
a butterfly?
the smell of fresh cut grass?
or the rain?

is it a rainbow?

but it can't be the pot at the end
capitalism masquerading as god
thinly veiled

but I see
because in this country of course
God is inventory
stocked in rows on shelves
with the goal of conformity
hurry
buy more stuff to be free

but there are some times
that I thought that I saw God

that day at the beach
when the heron flew over
just as the whale breached
and the sunset lit the sky
in glorious pinks

or the day in black block
standing shoulder to shoulder
with our most vulnerable neighbors
saying if you take one of us
you have to take all of us
and somehow none of us were taken

was that divine intervention

or was it just the way the rain poured down
and the cops stayed in their cars
as an elder passed around a piece of deer jerky
one bite each
giving us sustenance to outlast them
for one more hour

maybe the rain and God are the same thing?

but who is God?

is it someone granting me serenity
if I go to enough twelve step meetings
if I just climb to the twelfth step
surely a God will appear
in my God box
or wrapped around the coin
that counts the days of my abstinence

or if I tie my black belt just right
do my kung fu forms
finding peace of mind
the chi swirling around me
must contain some kind of God

is God the voice that whispers to me
deep in meditation?
or the things that I know
without knowing I knew them?
a container to hold all of my grievances?
someone to listen when I can't sleep at night
or the peace of mind that comes from
chanting the Hanuman Chalisa?

because Hanuman comes to me in my dreams
bringing ancestral drum beats
from this land
the land that I stand on
that does not belong to me
or him

the tie being that Hindu deities
also stolen by colonial genocide
white washed
and sold back to me
through the white yoga industrial complex

I reached for one

but I was told cultural appropriation

so I put it back

because I believe in
Indigenous rights
and Indigenous lives
and please give the land back
but if I don't know what land I come from
what God can I have?

maybe just a small God

one that comes from my own breath
the bottom of the exhale
the space inbetween

the nothingness that is spaciousness
filling in between everything

or something to put in my pocket
too small to be seen
but bigger than everything

a giant God
an enormous God
the sun

the moon
the stars stretching across the sky
some great phenomenal being
that no one dares defy

Allah
Buddha
Krishna
but does God even still like to be called God?
what if that's a dead name?

do they prefer higher power, spirit, nature,
almighty, holy ghost

or are they mother Gaia?
mother Earth?

but how can my God be something that's dying?

is God just a test
to see what I'll do
when never again becomes again right now
and we start railroading people
across state and international lines

does God respect my trans family?
and do they know
whose lives matter?
because black lives matter
and I will not accept a God
who doesn't put their own life on the line

and what kind of God
made a world
where we have to put our own lives on the line
for basic human rights
isn't God also bound by creed or covenant?
do they believe in

interdependence
pluralism
justice
transformation
generosity
and equity

love?

or are they beyond that?

are they just a flame on a chalice?
have they been extinguished
when dark times come?
can we relight them?
do they come from us?

or are they the light we must follow?
something bigger than us
a river flowing through us

is God love itself?
holding us
a hand reaching out
when I didn't know that I needed one
one more chance when I thought I was done

do we have to find them?
or are they always there?
and we just have to let them in?

maybe
God is not a place to arrive at
but a process
in which I seek and find
some semblance of meaning

and reverence for life

and I realize
I don't need to know
my God's name or face

maybe
they are some
or all
or none
of those things

but I'll still recognize them
when I see them again

American Dream

(March)

when I see people
still chasing the American dream
I just want to scream

I mean

I know you are all drugged up
on sugar and caffeine
but still
can't you see?

people now fearing fascism
but still revering its cousin capitalism
the two so intertwined
they both live
or they both die

both just addiction to power and money
turning human beings
into machines
parasitic things
with toxic schemes

killing dreams
and reams and reams of living things

depleting the earth
the soil
the water
the air
extracting and exploiting

just so a few people can
become billionaires

those in the middle
not realizing
what they are jeopardizing
and that a million dollars
is not something to aspire to
but something to set fire to
we must overcome the desire to
take more than what we need
override the programmed greed

those on the bottom
are the only ones that see
and we are too busy surviving

nobody is thriving

well you know who is thriving?
ticks are thriving

and one bite will give you lyme disease
and mosquitos bringing hydrocephalus
and viruses mutating
and cancers infiltrating
the balance everywhere reshaping

the earth now shaped
by daily rape

for our consumer ways
the droughts are staying
and it's always flooding
when it's raining
there is no abstaining
we are forced into participating
the microplastics in our bodies
never disintegrating
we are all self medicating

but shaming

those on opioids
who are also
just trying to cope with it
being choked by it
going broke in it
being woke back into it
by narcan rushing through

and that's the best we can do?

so I'm pleading with you
PLEASE
let's work together
to create something new

because resistance is justified
when people are occupied

and guess what
the system LIED
in order to divide us

we can try to hide
but so many people

plants and animals
have already died
we have to decide
to create a revolution
and not wait for the government's solution

the people have to choose
or we loose
and stay pieces for them to use
covered up by propaganda on the news

the intersectional catastrophe
growing every day
mother earth warning us
in her own ways
that she will not sustain this oligarchy
and we should have divested yesterday

but the beauty is

when things burn and collapse
it gives new growth a chance
some flowers burn only
on scorched land
and some people learn

only after losing everything they had

the earth will regenerate
and cleanse itself of our pollution

the only question is
will we create our own extinction
or be part of the solution?

My Autism In Itself
(April)

my autism in itself
is a gift with complications

a unique way of seeing things
creative ways of being
natural critical thinking
intuitive dreams

and it's also

forgetting names
and not recognizing faces

panic attacks at unfamiliar places

difficulty with transitions
and unspoken expectations
and in certain situations

mutism

which is not just inability to speak

but anxiety driven
progressive paralysis
exacerbated by society's
shame based analysis

and the sensory challenges
flooding my brain's synapsis
always overheating
because it's so overwhelming
everything overstimulating

sometimes
forced into bed rotting
because the world is just too exhausting

ears so sensitive
I hear the clock ticking
and the electricity flickering
over that racket
it's hard to hear what you are saying
so I'm always lip reading

and the visual demands
mean I'm always squinting

and cleaning
and organizing
arranging things in a particular order
so it doesn't take up the space in my brain
needed for thinking

if I hold still
then I need to be stimming
feet tapping
fingers fidgeting

while I'm up here speaking
I'm always shifting
hands in my pockets
so you can't see my spinner ring spinning

if I hold still
my anxiety will override
my capacity to stand here
which I'm already barely tolerating

but my autism comes with some fun surprises
an aptitude for unicycling
memorizing poems before I finish writing them
dreaming of people I haven't met yet

and getting so excited in real life
when I find them

I take advice from the wind
and I speak with the trees
propagating plants wherever I go
the earth and I breathing in sync

and if it's my special interest or passion
I'll perform above average
given a little encouragement
I'll flourish and learn
internalize it
until it becomes part of me
people saying I'm talented

so in a traditional indigenous culture
I would do well
I'd be a fantastic hunter gatherer
shaman
healer
storyteller

but my autism in a capitalist society
is a recipe for disaster

it's paralyzing
not even realizing
I'm always camouflaging
without trying

forced to be a chameleon
shape shifter
destroying my soul
to fit in
blend in
bend myself
into what you want me to be
conformity
neuronormativity

things I can never actually be

the masks I wear
so stuffy and tight
never quite right
and by night
I'm always bleeding inside

forcing myself into your container

and then struggling to breathe
in the constraints I've been placed in

living life in a foreign language
learning code switching
people always asking me
what country I'm from
when my accent is just…
autistic!

with a deep sense of justice
that can't be shaken
I'm often mistaken
assuming pure intentions
when people are actually staking me out
for the taking

swinging between abusive situations
and living life in isolation

confusing
and contorting
the world always seems to be distorting

I hold on desperately to familiar things

ritual, routine
pattern recognition

repulsed by acquisition of material things
capitalism can't get its jaw in
no matter how hard it bites
my brain automatically rejecting its lies

so it despises me

portraying me as broken
I'm never chosen
and no spaces are meant for me

I've learned to be terrified
of being perceived

chronic invalidation
creating struggles I didn't have as a child

daily suicidal ideation
my brain ruminating
trapped in its own black and white thinking

the fear

when I read online
the average life expectancy might be 35

and everyday
I stay alive out of spite

an act of resistance
against a system
that wants me to die

each time
I meet an autist older than me
it's a relief
someone made it through
maybe I can too

but what is the point
in a world
set on extinguishing my existence

but my autism in itself is delightful
finding simple things mesmerizing
empathic empathizing

small children recognizing

a friend in me

psychic visions I randomly see
my internal world always exciting

unlike the brain numbing droning
of one hundred therapists
explaining
the rudimentary psycho education
they always think
is going to fix me

but if anybody ever thought to ask me
I'm not looking for a cure
I wouldn't take a pill
magically making me allistic

I just want acceptance and inclusion
and to feel
and I am loveable
and my life has value
the way I am

as an autistic

Ocean Takes What It Wants

(May)

outside
it's the height of spring
with the promise of summer

but I think we all know
that right now it's actually dark winter that's
coming

we've all heard the music of Schindler's list
it goes on and on and on
that list so long

and now they are trying to remake it
with our names and our faces

I knew when I was a child
this moment was coming

because the ocean told me

I know you won't believe me
but it's true

my brothers and I
sitting in the sand
playing dare with the waves

you bury yourself up to your head
and wait for the tide to come in

it's daring
and scary
and thrilling

because coastal kids know
the ocean takes what it wants

and it also gives

gifts of polished rocks
and from the breadth of its depths
ancient wisdom
swept up and whispered
on its white caps
if you listen

and it fell in my ear

as it washed over me that day
THIS is what is coming

knowing it was coming
I've always tried
to do the right thing
be a cog
stop the machine

understanding intersectionality
before that was a catch phrase
standing with all people
and fighting for all of their needs

but I knew it WAS coming

so I don't know why I thought
we could stop it
I guess in good conscience
I just had to try

but now that it's here
I went to the coast
and I asked the ocean
okay, now what am I supposed to do?

and I thought it would say
get stronger, be braver
fight harder
make big crashing waves like me
but instead
it showed me its own softness
a flat clear sea
the waves quiet
gently lapping at my toes
patiently calming
and re-regulating me

and I understood it to say:

put your phone down
let the emails wait
clock in a little bit late
take time to see the beauty of the earth
while the earth is still beautiful
plant seeds while the soil is still viable
drink while the water is still drinkable

and yes
also dissent

while things are still dissentable
and fight
while battles are still fightable

but this moment in time
is also the time
to be quiet
silent
go inside
listen to your intuition
and dreams
meditate

people say
meditation
is to stay in the present moment
but the awakening is beyond that
it's timeless

reaching back for our own ancestors
and those of the Kalapayan people
whose land that we stand on

and forward in time
to my generation's

great great great granddaughters
unborn
but speaking to us
through the ethers

and out into the universe
and the earth
the water
the mountains
the trees
and to the tiniest forms of life
you can't even see

and to the spirits
and prayers
and songs
all the things beyond us

when we understand
and reclaim
the connections between all of us

universal consciousness

is when we rise above

this disease of disconnection
plaguing us
shaping us
into inhumane tyranny

because individually
we are each one drop
easily evaporable
and disposable

but together
we are the ocean
unmovable
unstoppable
capable of reshaping lands
and grinding boulders
into tiny grains of sand

if you are a very strong swimmer
you might swim in the Pacific
but if you get caught
in the undercurrent
of the riptide
you have to let go
and go along for the ride

take a deep breath
and prepare to go under

so breathe

while the air is still breathable
and love
while love is still definable

but don't take this as permission
for spiritual bypass
you can't sit in your privilege
and say
"I'm doing my part by going to yoga class"

this country was founded
on colonial imperialism
and you can't build something great
on a rotten foundation

and anyway
even the grandest sandcastles
are eventually taken out by the waves
the ebb and flow of the tides
civilizations come and they go

this moment in time is already past
and it hasn't happened yet
we are all majestic and free
wise and timeless

that's what the ocean told me

The First Pride Was A Riot

(June)

as you know
the first pride was a riot

a black trans woman
daring to stand up in defiance
recognizing,
it was the time and the place
to fight for queer rights

no hesitation

without stipulation
the only limitations
our own
confusion
and illusions

shaped by the constructs
of the closets
and the lines
and the boxes
that we have been kept in

but they do not define us
and we can loosen them

with persistence
and resistance
pushing back against a system
that has lied to us

tried to redesign, reassign
and ostracize us

falsely convicting us
as a means to lock us away

thinking

the anticipation
of incarceration
will keep us silent
and compliant

and eventually
we will just fade out
and go quietly away

but they don't know

that the thing about queer people is
we can not be contained

when restrained
we duplicate and multiply
replicate and reidentify

strategize

to become
gayer and queerer
and louder and stronger

when they come to take
or indoctrinate us
is when we throw
the biggest
loudest
gayest
celebrations

because we are not contagious

but our hope and our joy is
and THAT is the resistance
fueling our liberation

and YOURS
is also chained to us

so don't think

our resilience
is an excuse
to recuse
yourself from allyship

because in the current circumstance
we are overwhelmed & terrified
paralyzed
fearing for our lives

intertwined
with the responsibility
of visibility
keeping hope alive
for the next generation

four years is FOREVER
to a trans child

bringing heightened risk of suicide
while also fighting off a genocide
we will not concede
to this fascist tide
that is one hundred percent
intent
on eradicating us
their hate filled with ignorance

we dissent

unapologetic
embracing our identities
not acquiescing to authorities

so let it storm and rain

we will dance and sing
protest and chant
dressed in our gayest attire
protected by forcefields of solidarity

the whole queer community sticks together

our connection
a reflection
of our insistence
on existence

and after the storm
comes a rainbow
colors so bright
pride illuminating
lighting the night

if they cage us
WE will free us

still whole
hearts open
to love who we love
and be who we are meant to be

will you also fight for us
use your privilege to get rights for us
and if they come for us
stand in front of us

because they can't take all of us

but they can take a lot of us
if bystanders don't defy it

but we will always come back
intact
stronger
bolder
living older
re-igniting
and spreading like wildfire
we will never be smoldered

we are here
and we are queer

if you don't like it
expect a riot

Stuck In The Rabbit Hole

(July)

When I was a young teenager, I played Alice in a theatre production of *Alice in Wonderland*. I realized just recently that when I went down that rabbit hole, maybe I forgot to come back up again, because that would explain why the world is so topsy turvy and nothing seems quite right.

The Jabberwocky says:

"Twas brillig, and the slithy toves
Did gyre and gimble in the wabe:
All mimsy were the borogoves,
And the mome raths outgrabe."

But also like:

expectations written in the air
dissipating before I can see them
reading between lines
having to look people in the eyes
words that never match actions

voices silenced
things unable to be spoken
wrapped in shells
worn on the neck of sea witches

itty bitty eyes
and a great big smile
Cheshire cat
Rumplestiltskin
needle in a hay stack
discomfort of a pea
under 500 mattresses

the screech of cicadas
circadian rhythms
conversations with artificial intelligence

queens that shout "off with your head"
small children listening to that before bed

walking on eggshells
walls to sit on
and fall from
putting yourself back together again

all the kings horses
and all the kings men
couldn't make world peace
so why are they still the leaders then?
water, water everywhere
and not a drop to drink
excess food
excess famine

silkworms
pufferfish
jubjub birds
fireflies
the quiet footsteps
of the bandersnatch

chattering singing
of the flowers
under dripping sun
as rain lights the world

clouds around our feet
puddles in the sky
storms
green light

grass always looking greener
on the other side

weeds growing out of cement cracks
volunteer tomatoes
willing
but unable
under the wrath of lawn mowers

preferring manicured lawns
manicured nails
the latest fashions
polarities contained
inside of outdated systems

unearned privilege
needless suffering
loneliness in a crowd of billions

pied piper
following the people
who are following
self appointed leaders
who are among the sheep
counting themselves to sleep

chains meant to be broken

illusions
distortions
candle in the wind
purple rain
this little light of mine
hearts worn on the outside
even in dangerous times

fidgets for the mind

Wilbur in the web
Charlotte in the stall

Geppetto
Pinocchio
if only lies were visible
so we could see them all

mirror mirror on the wall

show me
the glacier peaks of Kilimanjaro

and deep pools
with water so clear
you can see the bottom

the birth of new life
death
incurable diseases

ring-a-round the rosie
pocket full of posies
ashes

ashes to ashes
dust to dust

pull from thin air
a tumtum tree
as high as Rapunzel's tower
hang a hammock
to break the fall
when the braid comes off

hope all our blinders do too

white rabbit

mirage
infatuation
temptation
thoughts in our own heads

we matter not at all
and we matter a great deal

what is this poem about?
I have no idea!

Ghost Of A Person

(August)

with a hidden disability
and unmet support needs
I'm unable to participate fully in life
but I'm not allowed to die either
so I hover on the outside
just a ghost of a person

a haunted existence

people say ghosts have unfinished business
mine is my whole life
waiting mistaken
thinking I'll grow into it

I go to things
but sit apart
separated from the best parts
the connection

seeing things other people miss
but I'm unable to touch them

understanding things other people forget
but I'm unable to speak them
I watch you silently
trying my best
to pretend
I'm also a person

people look right through me
unseen
ignored
until someone dares to perceive me
and screams for an exorcist

then
everyone staring at me

like I'm a freak abomination
some demonic variation
begging for attention
until I question my own reflection
floating adrift
aching in desperation
for the unattainable connection

an entourage of shattered dreams

trailing along behind me
all ripped apart
and badly sutured

straddling between realms
trapped in this body
but I don't belong here either

following along

dragging
crawling
stalled out on the floor
sobbing

and people walk right over me

not noticing or caring
zero empathy
for what I might be experiencing

contrasted
with the looks of horror
on people's faces
when they do happen

to see me coming

the toxic shame of that
seeping into me
poisoned and bleeding
trying to do anything
to keep from being perceived

but the simultaneous need to be seen
forcing myself into being
screaming
and pleading
can't anyone help me please

in between those two things
I float in a nowhere state
a citizen of no land
I wonder the world alone

just a ghost of a person

Fall Connotations

(September)

fall is a fickle lover
still holding the fingertips of summer
while chasing after winter

keeping its options open

with frosty mornings
followed by hot afternoons
embracing the rain
even as it's still kissing the sun

we pile all the layers on
and then take them off again
one by one

and it looks at us like
maybe we are the indecisive ones

fall
is when we fall back

an hour back in time

back to routine
back to school
little kids
all spruced up
in new clothes
and new shoes

too heavy backpacks
that carry the weight of the world

tiny shoulders
bent over
with summer hunger
and lunch debt rules

learning the most important things
are to sit quietly for hours
and walk single file in straight lines

training the next shift of workers
to be compliant
and accept overtime

we start to go inside

bringing in the last of the harvest
food shelves stocked full
next year's seeds drying in paper bags
garlic braids
hopeful green tomatoes
on the window sills

pumpkins set out in rows
waiting for hollows eve
day of the dead
calling in spirits
and dressed up friends
little ghosts & witches
princesses
and super heroes

collecting sweet treats
did you know
Americans eat
35 million pounds
of corn candy a year

corn rows
and corn mazes
hay rides

and cider presses

apple cider
apple juice
apple pie
the scraps fermenting
into vinegar
percolating
into ideas
that seep into our minds

an understanding that
we are all running on a staircase to nowhere

so how will we know when we get there?

and we think
we will do something about that later
when we have more time
maybe in winter

fall brings
prayed for rains
cleansing smoke filled skies
and making the air breathable again

just in time for
a month of gratitude practice

if the gratitude is real
it grows roots to anchor us
against autumn wind storms
and grounds us enough
to look at the truth of
how our country was born

Mayflower is a pretty name
but now we stand on bloody land
our hands stained

covered up by pumpkin spice
foam whipped coffees
and everything nice

woodstove lit for the first time this year
feet up
cats on my lap
good book by my side

just biding my time

waiting for a different kind of fall
one that frees us all

fall is a transitionalist
giving us time to stretch
into things we are uncomfortable with

a time when
so many things are dying back
but it is beautiful
in its crimson hues

depressing afternoon sunsets
but also
brilliant harvest moons

fall teaches us
not to be afraid
while descending into darkness
because it shows us
that there won't be darkness
without light

Witch

(October)

my great grandmother
lived until
I was in middle school
and after she died
for a while
she came to me in my dreams
taking the form of a squirrel

and she would tell me things

our ancestors she met
that had been burned at stake
and how, like her
I would be spared that
but only by the times
that prefer a constant slow burn
while keeping people alive

and she was right

so many reasons you can be staked
a little bit different

a little bit unique
red hair
freckles
strong intuition
forward telling dreams
the impulse to speak

they fear our strength
fear our softness
the combined power of that

feral
awake
worshipping only our ancestors
the breath of the earth
the rise of the moon

drawing outside the lines
pushing boundaries
no ordinary hours
dismissing the concept of time
whispering between realms
stretched between lives

sensitive

empaths
dreamers
creators
healers
the midwives
breathing things into being

speaking the sins
of those who wronged us
we feel the storms coming
and they think we conjured them

and for that
scape goated
pushed into the hollows
where coventries form
and spells
are sung as rhymes
binding
blurring lines

spirited
and willful
sleeping with eyes open
we become hard to crawl into

and would be perpetrators
find themselves
beckoned to

step
inside
the
circle

if they dare to

they will be cared for
seduction of reason
medicine makers
chanting
cauldrons over fire
with a thick fog of chamomile tea
lulling them to sleep

but they think
poison
bones
sisters of the devil
cursed in reincarnation

the power of love scares them
so they demand persecution

and we are misunderstood
misinterpreted
purposely misled
slayed
and executed
but they forget
we manifest as black cats
on Friday the 13th
and the crows are our friends

sly and sultry
bleeding femininity
life contained within

chanting incantations
unhindered by
the borders of this world
because we know others
conduits of destiny

mobilizing
soaring

beyond their reach
when they cage us
our spirits fly free

broomsticks optional
big hearts optimal

nothing without magic
can reach us

souls unburnable
believes uncorruptable

rejecting the language
of the colonizers
recognizing
no means no

the heart beat
of a witch on a stake
is unstoppable

rebirthed
into granddaughters
with unbridled tongues

brewing dangerous thoughts
controlling the night
paying reverence
to rituals
mysterious and secretive
candle lit remedies
that sooth
tarred and feathered pasts

unbothered
by the cowardness
of those who persecute us
for they are alive
without living
but we live on
even in death
souls unleashed upon this earth
to taunt them

and I smile

hoping my great grandmother
can see
what a scary thing
I've become

living alone with my books
in my garden
reciting these words
that magically appear in my head
to my only companions
two familiars
my cats

and I know
she would smile back at that

You Named Me America

(November)

you named me America

even though I already had a name

given to me by my people
those who know me
see me
have breathed collective breaths with me
for thousands of years

burying ancestors that become my soil
and we
live as one

America

sounds foreign to my ears
tastes bitter on my tongue
and bitter earth is never in your favor

named after one man
as if a man has right to claim land

any more than
a man has right to claim pieces of his mother

but you piece me off
into the shapes of your fantasies
scarring my body
with walls and fences
that don't belong there

"check mate"
you say
but the thing is
I wasn't playing

because I don't have a king

and you were never meant to have one either

foolish rulers
tripped up on pride
paying homage only to yourselves
my patience with you wearing thin
anger pouring into the cascadia subduction zone
so it won't be long

silly etch a sketch people
one shake
and you will be gone

but you never look at your own fault lines
those are erupting all of the time
because you don't know how to quell
the intolerable things that you feel
so you take

from anyone and everything
in attempt
to fill that well

renaming
things that already have names

Kalypuya, Multnomah, Nustucco,
Mt. Tahoma, Duwamish, Salish Sea

laying claim
to carve them for meat on your plate
not caring who else grows thin

damming the salmon

even after
a bereft mother
shows you her starved to death baby
for weeks

Tahlequah

as we know her
life giver
auntie, sister
celestial mother
relative to us all
but you call her
J35

because numbers are meant to dehumanize
and if you don't give her personhood
you think
you don't have to save her

but she is me
and I am you
all of us woven together
we feel what the others feel
you

just won't acknowledge it

we are fire
we are wind
we are rain

and a scale of one to ten
no longer
contains our pain

we are now wounds that do not heal
screams that never cease
we are hungry in the gardens
thirsty in the rivers
choked by nooses
made from your isms
liabilities, debts and collateral

that do not need to be here

I am life itself
humbly offering you
the milk of my breasts
and you rape me
even as you drink it

say my name

I am Kheya Wita
Unci maka

Pachamama
Turtle island

I am paradise

but
America
was never great

Anxiety

(December)

my anxiety
is a thing that stays with me all of the time
an imp that sits on my chest
drumming and drumming
as fast as she can
in rhythms that I don't understand

her brother
a thief
stealing my breaths
one at a time
until there is not enough left
even to cry

cry cry cry

my anxiety is an echo
that repeats in my head
telling its own story
over and over and over again

I'm anxious I'm anxious I'm anxious

stuck in a pattern
that loops in my mind
going around and around and around
getting louder and louder
until I say it outloud

I'm anxious I'm anxious I'm anxious

I opened my mouth
why did I say it?
I should have stayed quiet
I'm breathing too loud

loud loud loud

I try to stay right on the rails
precariously balancing
but blowing around
there is not enough water for swimming
but I'm always drowning

drowning drowning drowning

I can't even make it through the day

the lights are too bright
and there are people around
watching me
too close behind me
trying to be nice to me

me me me

I try to reach out
but I don't know if I can
maybe I shouldn't
and anyway
I'm shutting down

down down down

my anxiety is wasps
swarming inside of me
intolerable feelings I really can't stand
voices in my head telling me
I'm bad

bad bad bad

I'm going to die

die die die

I gotta get out of here now

now now now

running as fast as I can
but I'm frozen inside
and in time
a second an hour
an hour a second

I'm anxious I'm anxious I'm anxious

my anxiety is sometimes
a flat affect face
with a painted on smile
doing the best that I can
one breath at a time

About the Author

Tristan Elliott is a Pacific Northwest Native, having grown up on the Oregon coast, living most of her adult life in Seattle, WA, and currently residing in Eugene, OR.

Tristan wrote her first spoken word piece in January 2025 and made her debut appearance at a mic in March of 2025. Since then she has performed at over 40 events and shows no sign of stopping!

Connect with Tristan directly at tristanelliott.com